Seasons, Spells and Magic

WINTER

by
Tudorbeth

Seasons, Spells and Magic

WINTER

By Tudorbeth

Published by Tudor Publishing - United Kingdom
www.TudorPublishing.com

Copyright © Tudorbeth and Tudor Publishing 2016. All rights reserved.

ISBN 978-1-326-73834-1

FIRST EDITION

For the purposes of all permissions licenses and agreements relating to this publication the written permission of the copyright owners or their designated agents must be in hard copy form and not electronic. Emails are not considered valid and will be classed as null and void for legal purposes. Any prior arrangements to excerpt use or quote this material is hereby rescinded under the new copyright ownership and new digital formats of the material. No part of this book may be reproduced in any form. This book is licensed to the purchaser for personal use only with all rights reserved. No part of this publication may be reproduced or stored in a retrieval system, copied, duplicated or transmitted in any form, or by any means, electronic, mechanical, photocopying, recording, internet, computer or used for presentation and demonstration purpose or otherwise without the express prior written permission of all copyright owners or in the case of reprographic production, in accordance with the terms of licenses issued by the Copyright Licensing Agency.

No part of this material may be used for excerpt purposes without the prior written permission of the copyright owners and any references to this publication must be accompanied by proper reference and due credit must be given to both the source www.TudorPublishing.com the publication and the copyright owners.

No part of this publication may be circulated in any form or binding or cover other than that in which it is published and without a similar condition being imposed on the subsequent purchaser.

Tudor Publishing - United Kingdom
http://www.TudorPublishing.com

Further books to come in this Series:

Seasons, Spells and Magic - SPRING
Seasons, Spells and Magic - SUMMER
Seasons, Spells and Magic - AUTUMN
Tudorbeth's Mini Book of Spells
Sea Magic and Spells
English Magic and Spells
Scottish Magic and Spells
Irish Magic and Spells
Welsh Magic and Spells

DISCLAIMER

The material contained in this book is for information purposes only, being esoteric in nature. It is not intended to be a medical guide or a manual for self-treatment. The information represented in this book is not intended to be a substitute for medical counselling or treatment prescribed by your doctor. It is not intended to diagnose, treat or cure any disease or treat any individual's health problems or ailments.

This book is sold with the understanding that the publisher and the author are not liable for the misconception, misinterpretation or misuse of any information provided.

In the event you use any of the information in this book for yourself, which is your constitutional right, the publisher and author assume no responsibility for your actions with respect to any loss, damage, or injury caused or alleged to be caused directly or indirectly by the information contained in this book.

The intent of the author is only to offer the information contained in this book to help you in your quest for information about the subject.

If you have, suspect to have or are suspected to have a medical problem, we advise you to seek competent professional medical advice and assistance.

Contents

Seasons Blessing	8
Introduction	9
The Pentagram of Alchemy and Seasonal Magic	13
Winter	17
The Winter Garden	26
The Winter Crystal	30
Snow and Ice Spells	33
December	47
A Midwinter Wedding	64
: Ceremony	67
: Wedding Feast	70
: Wedding Menu	72
: Wedding Recipes	74
January	80
Divination by Runes	86
Spells and Charms	93
February	107
Spells and Charms	109
Conclusion: The Seasonal Witch	123
Winter Calendar of Festivals	126
Dictionary of terms and festivals throughout the year	129
Online Course – Wicca 101	130
Witchcraft Course – First Degree Level	133
How to Find out More	140
Bibliography	141
Other Books	146

Seasons Blessing

Summer, Autumn, Winter and Spring.
Blessed be to the Turning of the Wheel.
Let me embrace all the good you bring.
All the seasons' changes I will feel.
Peace and love in every month in every day.
In every rain drop, in every snowflake that comes my way.
Glory to the scorching sun, glory to the breeze.
I am grateful to the cool summer seas.
To rainbows and storms blessed be.
To the Turning of the Wheel.
Summer, Autumn, Winter and Spring so mote it be.

Introduction

Magic is the real force in all of us although at times we can find it hard to believe in ourselves and therefore believe in our own magic. Yet it is there for as beings of the Divine it lingers within us waiting to be released. Magic is a force that surrounds us, that penetrates us and that we are a part of. Throughout the seasons it is easier to see magic as the magic of nature screams at us to notice its power and force. We must respect nature and honour the fierce magic within as we are also a part of this power.

This book shows how within the realm of magic seasons play a huge part as does Alchemy. Alchemy is the scientific study of magic. Alchemy was the precursor to our natural sciences of today such as Chemistry and Physics. Alchemists 'holy grail' was the search to turn base metals such as lead into gold. Yet Alchemists were not only concerned with the physical properties of gold but with the actual spiritual content also. That metal was the spiritual 'metal' of human beings. Alchemists' goal was learning, understanding, science and belief, and their code was solution and coagulation.

Alchemists study everything in this world we can see and also that world we cannot see. Alchemists' symbols feature nature in all its glory from animals, birds, colours as well as parables and the archetypal symbols such as the Cosmic Egg. We owe a lot to the Alchemists of the past both in science matters and also our spiritual matters. The Alchemists world was one of magic and mystery. Here in this series you will see the Alchemical symbols that accompany each season.

Spring   Summer   Autumn   Winter

In the vast realm of magic, we can find not only Alchemy but the Tarot, Zodiac and the Divine in all its forms. In this series the Gods and Goddesses of our past are found and honoured within the seasons. Much has been written of our Turning of the Wheel and the festivals we find in the passing months. In this book we shall investigate the actual practical magic that flows through our seasons and the gods that rule over the months of the year. Moreover, each season is presided over by a set of deities therefore the Norse Gods and Goddesses have authority over the winter months. While spring is presided over by Celtic deities, summer is Greek and autumn is Roman.

The world is going through a transition and we can see stories of the gods appearing in films and in music. The gods are returning to us though in truth they have never really left. Their everlasting presence is felt constantly in the arts their true home. We are responding to that again now with so much happening in our world. Those of us who have been

practitioners of Wicca and followers of nature know this and now that knowledge is once again coming to the fore.
This book shows some of the ways ancestors understood the seasons in particular the winter with its harsh weather. Yet with magic they could go about their daily lives. The mysteries of the Northern Lights dancing across the winter skies over a frozen landscape must appeared as the Gods themselves riding their chariots across the world. Whilst the

frost sweeping down from the mountains and across the landscape must for all intents and purposes appeared like frost giants swallowing the world.

Traditions, spells, potions and magic were used to counteract the harsh weather. The philosophies, rules and ways were passed along through oral tradition from generation to generation and finally written down. It is the old ways you find here. The recipes, beliefs and sayings for a winter season can be found among these pages. That magic and knowledge of the ancestors is still within you.

The Pentagram of Alchemy and Seasonal Magic

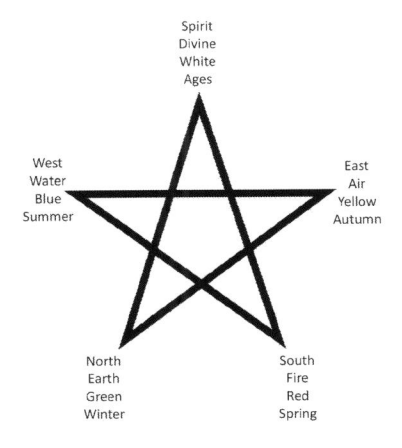

```
              Spirit
              Divine
              White
              Ages

West                              East
Water                             Air
Blue                              Yellow
Summer                            Autumn


    North                  South
    Earth                  Fire
    Green                  Red
    Winter                 Spring
```

The old practioners had no doctrine or creed. They lived their lives among the raw beauty of nature. They did not turn west to cast a spell at 7.32pm. The ancestors did not have digital watches! They had Stonehenge, New Grange or Long Meg. Their measurement for time was the seasons themselves. The shortest day or the longest days were their clocks. These phases of the sun and moon told them the passing year. The changes in the seasons told them when to plant, when to sow, when to hunt and when to stock up on firewood. The times when crows build their nests high in the trees would indicate the coming summer would be a good one. If the Hawthorne was laden with berries, then the coming winter would be harsh.

Anything at all in nature you can use in your Craft and spell work. Witches are beings of nature. Therefore, we can use everything in nature. Though we must show respect and honour all in this world and not abuse the power we have been given. Always abide by the Wiccan Rede:

> An it harm none, do what ye wilt.

The Rede is the only doctrine, the only rule we have. So in your magical work always abide by it. Seasonal magic is the beginning of all magic. Shamans and witches always had power over the elements and seasons, weather spells are nothing new. Indeed, in the past it was precisely for this reason why so many of us were persecuted, allegedly for interfering in the weather. However, in this book we shall learn how to weave the elements and to embrace the magic of nature.

Every aspect of the seasons and their magic will be discussed. Including working with the elementals themselves, such as Will-o-the-Wisp and other sprites shall be referred to.

In order to work alongside these series of books the only resources you need are a pen and a notebook, and YOU. You are the most important part of this book as without YOU there is no magic.

It is with this in mind that all the spells and life ceremonies referred to in this book are exemplars. Magic grows as we grow. It is individual yet connected to all. Therefore, mould the magic into your life. In the beginning nothing fits perfectly, a new pair of shoes need wearing before they feel comfortable and magic is no different. Try the spells and use the ceremonies but stretch them till they feel right for you.

This book embraces all that is in nature, all that we can see and all that is unseen. This book, the first of four, takes winter on a magical journey. We will look at the festivals of that season, the weather, and the spells attached to them. We shall look at the important ceremonies regarding the key stages of life such as marriage, birth and death.

So let us begin our journey of magic and enchantment with winter and the Gods of the north.

Blessed Be.

Winter

'Plenty of holly berries predict a cold winter'

Winter is a season of wondrous delights. There are so many festivals and joyful occasions in winter that it is anything but quiet. Although on dark, damp cold days we want nothing better than to stay indoors and hibernate like some of our animal friends do. We can feel the sleeping magic that is all around us building up to burst anew in spring. Yet magic is not sleeping, one could argue that in winter, magic is more alive than in any other season.

The months of winter; December, January and February traditionally in the northern hemisphere bring with them snow, frost, wind, winter storms, icicles. The winter also brings freezing rain, which can slap you so hard you feel as though you have been hit by Gaia herself. Yet within the harsh brutality of this season there is magic all around from the smallest snowflake, which reminds us how unique yet connected we are. Every snowflake though all are different all has six points.

On dry cold winter nights Jack Frost paints our city streets and gardens with his glistening white magic. He forms icicles and creates works of art out of our cars and trees. Yet through all its harshness the winter also brings light and life reminding us constantly how connected we are to the changing seasons.

Few plants flower in the winter yet those that do are some of the most fragile and beautiful one of any season. Yet despite their fragile beauty they are the strongest flowers nature gives us. When we look at the purity of snow white snowdrops or the vibrant yellow of winter aconites we realise what strength nature has. To the blessing of tiny Glory of the Snow, blue and white star shaped flowers, which also have six points like the snowflake. The deep purple of the crocus or the bell shaped Pasque. Further, let us not forget the Christmas Rose who flowers in the middle of winter in shady, frost free spots with its dark evergreen leaves that can stand the winter cold.

The winter in the northern hemisphere is both beautiful and brutal. It can bring our modern cities to a standstill and suddenly we are surrounded by the still quiet of winter. Airports close and we see the sky without planes darting here and there. It is in these rare moments of complete silence that we can feel the magic. The Goddess is all around us. The world is white, still and breathing silently while catching its breath in a winter wonderland. It is here we can tap into the magic of this beautiful season and give thanks while performing our own magic.

As this is the season of winter the deities that dominate the winter months are the Norse Gods and Goddesses. The Celtic deities shall come into the end of the season with February customs and traditions. The people of the north shall feature in this season. There are many Gods and Goddesses in the northern pantheon. However, we shall concentrate on the main ones for the purposes of the forthcoming spells.

We will look at the corresponding festivals of that month and learn some old and some new spells. The deities that preside over winter are the Gods and Goddess of the north: Odin, Thor, Freya and the Valkyries.

There are many Norse gods and goddesses who are then divided by categories of either warrior gods or fertility gods. Also within this pantheon of the Nordic divine we find elves, dwarves and Jotner or frost giants and the Valkyries, warrior women who help fallen soldiers onto Valhalla.

There are many Gods and Goddesses in the Nordic pantheon but the ones we are most familiar with are Baldr who is the God of beauty, peace, innocence and interestingly rebirth, while Eir is the Goddess of healing. Freya is the Goddess of love, fertility and beauty. The matriarch of the Nordic divine is Frigg or Frigga who can be compared to the Greek Goddess Hera as Frigga is the Goddess of marriage and motherhood. The wonderful trickster God Loki is the God of mischief and general naughtiness. Yet the male father God we all know is Odin who is the ruler of the Gods and Father of All. Odin is often associated as part of a trinity; Odin, Vili, Ve. The trinity or triad in the Nordic creation myths created the first human couple. Odin gave life and the soul to the couple. While Vili gave intelligence and the sense of touch and Ve gave speech, hearing, and sight. Odin, Vili and Ve are brothers, with Odin being the eldest and ruler of all. Vili is the middle and Ve is the youngest brother. The triad is often cited as Spirit, Will, and Holiness. As each of these Gods represent inspiration, will or desire and spiritual power or the numen.

However, the Nordic God we probably are all aware of is Thor, Odin's eldest son. Thor is the God of Thunder and is able to yield the power of lightening due to his hammer, which is a symbol of strength and courage. Any spells you do regarding Thor or asking for his help is always best done on a Thursday which some call Thor's Day. Though by far the God skiers will identify with is Ull, the God of Skill. Today some professional skiers may have his symbols on their ski gear as he is also the God of Skiing as well as the God of Marksmen. Here is a specific chart for correspondences of the Norse Gods and Goddesses. It can be used all year or just for the winter months. It is entirely your choice how you would like to work with the Norse Divine.

Chart of Norse Deities

Day	Colour	Deity	Tree	Crystal
Sunday	Gold	Sol	Yew	Gold Stone
Monday	White	Mani	Hawthorn	Moon Stone
Tuesday	Yellow	Tyr	Pine	Red Jasper
Wednesday	Blue	Odin	Ash	Diamond
Thursday	Red	Thor	Oak	Emerald
Friday	Green	Freya	Lime/Linden	Amber
Saturday	Silver	Loki	Wych Elm	Norwegian Moonstone (Laravkite)

Winter is associated with the north. In the Tarot the north is represented by the suit of Pentacles which is the earth. To pull a Pentacle in a tarot reading signifies money, possessions and material wealth. It is also security, work and interestingly, values. The Pentacles can also be called the Suit of Coins in some tarot decks. Coins of course always represent money and trade. The colour is usually green for obvious reasons.

Green is often associated with magic itself and of course green also represents nature.

In the Zodiac the winter months are hosts to Sagittarius, Capricorn, Aquarius and the water babies of Pisces. From the beginning of winter with the fire sign of Sagittarius to the ending of winter and the coming of spring with the water sign of Pisces. Winter is a magnificent season of magic.

Magic is entwined so far into our everyday lives that we take it for granted. Therefore, we do not see the magic as clearly as we should. When surrounded by beauty every day we do not see it. We literally cannot see the forest for the magic of the trees.

In the winter despite its beauty the sun seems far away from us and we can begin to feel ill as a result. Many people are more and more beginning to suffer from Seasonal Adjustment Disorder and are prescribed to sit in front of light box. The seasons and their changes have such an effect on us. Yet none is more felt than in the winter months.

Winter's Morn Strength Spell

During the winter months our energy levels may wane. Thus with each passing week it gets harder and harder to be energised all the winter's day. We are faced with biting wind, cold damp conditions and numerous grey days. Life in the northern hemisphere can be incredibly draining!

Try this spell on a winter's morn. It is good if it's a sunny, snow day as that will give you an added boost but this spell works just as good on a grey day too. You will need an orange cut in half, and a yellow candle.

Light the yellow candle:

> Winter's morn, winter's day
> Send heat and light my way.
> Return to me my energy.
> An it harm none so mote it be.

Slice the half orange again to make quarters with your Athame, one for each season. Smell the orange, the zesty sweetness. Imagine as you begin to eat it the energy pouring into you as you look at the yellow candle. Feel the heat and then see the bright flame illuminating the day and you. Eat the orange and go about your day with a new energised spring into your step.

Magic and spells is about using all your senses. In the winter this is very true none more so than in the winter garden. The plants and trees of a winter garden have such gentle fragrances and delicate flowers that they are a delight to look upon.

The Winter Garden

The garden is alive in winter just as in the rest of the year. Trees feature very strongly in winter while most of them are sleeping there are some who are more alive in winter than in any other season. Some plants even flourish in the winter. Here is a selection of the best ones for a winter display. They are the winter garden pentagram of plants.

Daphne

A Daphne plant can fill a room with its scent and also makes a pretty winter display in the garden. One particular variety which has gained popularity is the Daphne Napolitana. While the Daphne Odora is called the winter Daphne, both are beautiful plants to have in a winter garden.

Sarcocca Hookeriana

The other plant that is perfect for a winter wonder garden is the Sarcocca Hookeriana. It is an evergreen shrub which produces beautiful white flowers throughout winter. It then develops black berries. The flowers are so sweet that no wonder the plant is also called the 'Himalayan Sweet Box,' for the flowers are simply divine. Though remember as they are white always ask the Goddess permission before cutting a sprig to bring indoors for a winter display.

Winter Viburnum

The Winter Viburnum is a beautiful plant to have in your garden. It delivers in both sight and fragrance. The clusters of pink flowers adorn its branches with a sweet smell. They begin pink then gradually turn white. Cut them for the house or midwinter wedding table decoration as cut flowers they can last for a long time.

The Winter Viburnum can flower all winter from October through to March. Viburnum Bodmanatense 'Dawn' is excellent and can be referred to as Freya's Flower. It is strong, hardy with deep green leaves. The clusters of scented flowers begin life as red buds then turn pink before finishing their life as white flowers. It is truly a beautiful plant to have in the garden. It is also perfect to have for a midwinter feast or wedding.

Crocus

The one flower that is most common during winter is the crocus. This delicate little flower can bloom in autumn, winter and spring depending on the species. The specie Crocus Laevigatus can start flowering in late autumn through winter and into February. So it is a good plant to have in the garden. Crocus Imperati is another variety that is good to have in your winter garden.

Lonicera Purpusii - Winter Beauty

This plant is often referred to as the Winter Honeysuckle. It is a delightful plant with delicate fragrant white flowers. It flowers in December and January. It is truly a Winter Beauty.

These five wonderful plants of such delicate beauty and gentle fragrance help us to remember that life and the Gods are always here. There must be a winter in order for the spring and subsequent summer to follow. The Nordic Gods and Goddesses would not leave the earth completely void of life and magic in the winter months. The Elves and Dwarves that dwell in the tree of the nine worlds are welcome in any garden of Midgard whatever the weather. So make them welcome by planting the trees and plants as described here. This is a garden blessing to attract the Elves and Dwarves of the Yggdrasil:

> Welcome Elves, welcome Dwarves.
> Welcome to beings of all.
> Enjoy my garden and bring your magic.
> But leave only good wishes for all.
> An it harm none so mote it be.
> Blessings to both you and me.

The Winter Crystal

Here in the winter months there is a particular stone that can work wonders. It is the snow quartz which was said to have come from the Goddess Hulda's icicle wand. She cast her wand over the land so that it may sleep and grow strong again for the coming spring. As such the snow quartz is good for slowing the pace of our frantic lives so that we might also rest and recuperate.

It is also good for a healing a rift in families. Further it is beneficial to keep a piece in your purse or handbag if there are financial difficulties. It is a stone which keeps good luck flowing.

Here is a Snow Quartz blessing:

> Blessed be to you snow quartz.
> The gifts you bring.
> Bless this love, bless this house.
> As sure as winter there is spring.
> For now and evermore so mote it be.

The Snow Quartz is the specific winter crystal yet there is another during this season which can be used. The amber is a stone of February as it is the stone of Freya. Amber is a wonderful crystal. It is fossilized tree resin and has been used for many millennia for its beauty and healing properties. It is often termed as the gold of the north.

Amber can come in many colours from the more common orange and brown coloured amber to red, green and even blue amber. The blue amber is extremely rare and is very precious. It appears blue almost a deep teal colour in normal sunlight and yet when held again sunlight becomes the common amber with yellowish, orange colouring. It is because of this fact that it is highly sought after by those who work in magic. It is used in glamour and transformation spells.

Amber spells feature in the February section and is used with Freya. However here is a special amber blessing spell to invoke the power of the stone to all your winter needs. Hold a piece of amber in your hands and say:

>   Blessed stone of winter's north.
>   I ask your powers come forth.

Bring to me all I desire.
Wealth, love and passion's fire.
Send your winter blessing to me.
An it harm none so mote it be.

Keep the stone in your purse or pocket for the duration of the winter months.

Snow and Ice Spells

Snow is magical full stop! It makes everything clean, bright, fresh and pure. We seem to be empowered with extra energy the moment it arrives. There are many spells that accompany snow. Snow is graceful and time honoured. There is a timeless quality to it which can be used for time spells. One of the many spells is one which captures that energy we feel when we wake up to a snowy bound house day. Normally, work would be shut, schools close, the traffic may have ground to a halt and it is a glorious snow day which is a day off purely for magic and loved ones.

> 'When the snow falls dry it means to lie;
> But flakes light and soft bring rain oft.'

This old saying is quite true as pavements and the earth dry up before a fall of snow and if the earth is dry the snow will settle. If however, the pavements are wet already the snow will simply melt when it lands. Though it is also worth remembering this saying when it comes to snow and predicting a snow storm.

'It takes three cloudy days to bring a heavy snow.'

The First Snows Spell

When there has been a forecast of snow take a clean plastic bowl or lunch box and place outside. We are trying to get as much as snow as possible. This spell is done with the first snow of the season but no matter if you have had several flurries previously.
Put the bowl or lunchbox outside and collect as much of the snow as possible. When it has stopped snowing or when the lunch box/bowl is full bring inside. In a freezer bag empty the snow and as you do say these words:

> Pure white snow, nature's innocence.
> White and clean shinning vibrance.
> Bring me your strength and purity.
> In all my magical endeavours.
> An it harm none so mote it be.

Put the freezer bag in the freezer after you have written on the bag 'magic snow' and date it. If it is the first snows mark on the bag '1st Snow,' to show that the snow has important and the purest of properties.

This snow can now be kept in the freezer and be used throughout the year for a number of spells. This snow can be used for anything from love to money to health.

Depending on what day the snow falls the energy of that day can be used to enhance the snow's power. All things connect in magic. Snow is the innocent and purest of magic. One on which we can put our own spells on. It is another of nature's resources that we can harness the power of.

Here is a list of correspondences of days, Gods and Goddesses, star sign, stone, and colour that can be used throughout the year. It is a generic list.

Day	Star Sign	Deity	Colour	Stone	Rules
Monday	Cancer	Diana	White	Moonstone	Home, politics, business, women's Power
Tuesday	Aries, Scorpio	Mars	Red	Ruby	Sex, passion, desire, ambition, work, competition
Wednesday	Gemini, Virgo	Mercury	Yellow	Opal	All forms of Communication, magical ability, knowledge, rational thought
Thursday	Sagittarius, Pisces	Jupiter	Orange	Amethyst	Luck, abundance, expansion, career
Friday	Taurus, Libra	Venus	Green	Emerald	Beauty, money, marriage, love, fertility
Saturday	Capricorn, Aquarius	Saturn	Black	Onyx	Karma, reincarnation, work, reality past lives
Sunday	Leo	Sun	Gold	Goldstone	Joy, happiness, health, leadership

You can download this image in the reader's resources at www.seasonsspellsandmagic.com

This is not exhaustive list there are many other correspondences associated with these days but it is handy to know some of them for spell casting. Therefore, write this out in your book of shadows, or write out onto a piece of card and laminate it and keep it as a book marker.

If you collect your snow on a Friday, then it can be used for money making spells. In a glass jar place some coins, the higher the denomination the better. Cover with your snow collected on a Friday. Then tie a green ribbon around the jar and say these words:

No Money Like Snow Money Spell

> Blessed be, thankful to thee.
> Goddess Freya on this Friday.
> From now till there again.
> Let this jar fill with money.
> An it harm none so mote it be.

Let the snow melt in the jar and on top of the money. You can do this spell on a Friday and keep it overnight until the next week when it is Friday again. Empty the jar of snow water and coins saying:

> Thankful to thee, blessed be.
> Thank you Goddess Freya.
> For now and evermore blessed be.

The snow money water can be kept in a spray bottle and use it for when you need a little extra financial boost. Spray a little round yourself on an endeavour for finances either a meeting with a bank manager or when you are asking your boss for a pay rise.

Snow Spell Charm

Make a snow spell charm. Take a green apple and thinly cut it across to expose the pentagram inside. Cut at least five very fine slices of the apple make sure they all have the pentagram in them. Then gather your money snow on a Friday. Lay the apple slices out on a plate and with your money snow sprinkle it over the apple slices. Say these words as you do:

> May these gifts of nature.
> Pure brilliant snow of winter bright.
> Charm these apple slices.
> With financial strength and might.
> Blessed Be.

Leave the apple slices on the plate for a full seven days. Until the apple slices have withered. They should look and feel a bit like leather. Then take one of the apple slices and put it in your purse, one in your bank book or wherever else you need or have other financial books such as cheque book and credit cards. Keep the apple slices in your financial places until you feel you no longer need them. Then bury them in the garden, giving thanks for all the good they brought.

Snow Wish Spell

Here is a lovely little spell to say when you want something. Make a wish upon the snow. Be out in the snow when you say this spell. Or use your first snow that you have kept in the freezer. Over the snow say this little spell:

> Snow light snow bright.
> Grant me a wish tonight.
> (Say what it is you wish for)
> An it harm none so mote it be.

You can this spell every night for seven nights until your wish comes true.

Snow Money Spell

Here is a little money spell for the snow. See if you can buy also a money tree to go along with this spell. There are two different types of money trees. One is also called the Jade Plant or Friendship Tree and whose Latin name is Crassula Ovata. It also produces small white or pink star like flowers in spring. The other money tree is called Pachira Aquatica and also called the Malabar chestnut. However the former is more commonly available as a houseplant.

Light a green candle on a Friday preferably and in front of your money tree say these words:

> Mighty snow light and pure.
> Of riches I want more.
> Send me money as if from trees.
> An it harm none so mote it be.

Snow Travel Spell

When travelling in the snow and ice it can be rather dangerous so before you embark on any type of journey say this spells. You can say this spell before beginning your journey or the day before. You can say it in the car or say it on the plane. If you have time and want to say it before then light a blue candle as you say these words:

> Shimmering snow.
> Safety please.
> Shimmering snow
> Here we go.

Bully Stop Snow Spell

As discussed previously the flowers that bloom in the winter months are some of the most fragile flowers of any season. Yet their strength to withstand the harshest of winds and frosts is simply outstanding. This spell draws upon the power and strength of the snowdrop to give you strength in times of need. This is particularly good spell to use if someone is bullying you at work or school, college or anywhere in any situation in which you are being undermined by someone.

Have a picture of a snowdrop or if you can do this spell outside near some wild snowdrops. Never on any occasion cut anything white in nature and bring it into the house. Everything white in nature belongs to the Goddess, and she is not happy when her flowers or plants are disturbed, so leave them be.

Look upon the picture of the snowdrop or out in the garden as you say this spell:

> Snow drop, snow drop.

Gentle and strong.

Give me strength to fight the one.

He/She tries to undermine me.

With cold words and harsh deeds.

Snow drop, snow drop.

Help me please.

An it harm none so mote it be.

Ice Spells

The winter weather brings gifts of not only snow and cold winds but also ice. Ice is the domain of Jack Frost and occasionally he will leave a special gift of icicles. Icicles are amazing they are nature's winter wand. They can vary in shape and size. If you are lucky enough to have icicles then thank Jack Frost for leaving the icicle for you and snap it off. Then wrap it in a freezer bag and leave it in your freezer.

Ice Wand Spell

The icicle is nature's wand and you can use it for all manner of magic works. You have no need for wands in magic, the magic is within you but if nature leaves you one then take it. It is a gift for and is an extension of your magic. Before you use your magic want say these words over it and then quickly put back in the freezer:

> Blessed water turned to ice.
> A gift from the winter night.
> Thank you Jack Frost.
> Let my wand full of magic be.
> An it harm none so mote it be.

Throughout the year you can use your wand for magic. With every spell you cast your wand will gradually reduce. When the wand has completely disappeared the magic has been spent from it.

Next we will look at some more spells that concern Jack Frost.

Jack Frost Money Spell

On some silver aluminium foil write the sum of money you require. Then fold the foil into three and sprinkle some sea salt over it. While doing so say these words.

> Jack Frost blessed be.
> Jack Frost please help me.
> Grant me this sum of money.
> An it harm none so mote it be.

Keep the foil in a safe place.

Jack Frost Soulmate Spell

Jack Frost might have a negative persona, granted he is not as cuddly as elves or fairies but no elemental should ever be taken as being gentle and sweet, they all have their moments! However, Jack Frost can help in matters of the heart. Please do not think his heart is as frozen as his art, nothing could be further from the truth.

Here is a little spell asking Jack Frost to help you in bringing your Soulmate closer to you. Light a silver candle anointed with mint oil. Make some mint tea and have it steeping near you as you say this spell. This spell is best done on a Wednesday.

> Jack Frost sprinkle your magic on me.
> Send me love of the one who is meant for me.
> Jack Frost blessed be.
> An it harm none so mote it be.

December

'At Christmas meadows green, at Easter covered with frost'

December in the Northern hemisphere can be a strange month as we can have snows and bitter frosts. Then on December 25 it can be so mild you can go for a walk on a beach, through a city park, or in the countryside wearing just your Christmas jumper! People even go swimming in the seas around Britain.

Yet the meaning of this saying says it all really for if it is mild at Christmas then we are likely to be freezing come Easter. Here in the Northern hemisphere one thing is certain we shall always have a winter it just depends what months it comes in as some Augusts have been colder than some Decembers.

Another saying similar to this is the saying concerning Christmas Day:

'So far as the sun shines on Christmas Day, so far will the snow blow in May'

For many of us December brings with it Christmas, lots of food, presents and sending greetings. Yet in our modern world this new festival had its origins in our pagan past. Saturnalia was the Roman mid-winter festival which honoured of Saturn, God of Corn and Harvest. It was a seven-day festival starting on 17th December and finishing on the 23rd December. To say it was a time of excess is an understatement.

We can relate so many of today's customs from it. Houses were decorated and presents were given and greetings sent. We today might complain about our Christmas dinners yet the meals of yesteryear lasted for at least eight or nine hours! Lots of merry making and drinking perhaps to drink and blot out the cold dark winter!

However, it is with another tradition that Christmas stems from which concerns us here. It is about the Gods of the north. The Norsemen's' belief was Jol or as we now know it Jul or Yule.

Jul was a twelve-day festival beginning in the Winter Solstice Eve. So from December 20th through to 31st December there was much feasting. Jul signified the end of all things with the solstice and the beginning as the light would return to the earth. After the Winter Solstice the nights would start to get longer. A minute longer goes onto the day light hours after the solstice. The full moon in December is often referred to as the Long Nights Moon.

Long Night Moon Healing Spell

Here is a spell which asks for the Long Night Moon for healing at this time of year. Light one white and one green candle. Say these words while imaging the sun returning to the land.

> Long night blessed night.
> Heal me well and right.
> Winter's hold over land and me.
> Sun now returning blessed be.
> Winter release your hold and set me free.
> Let the land awaken and sun heal me.
> An it harm none so mote it be.

Keep the candles lit for as long as possible before either allowing them to burn out naturally or extinguishing them.

At Jul the Wild Hunt was said to be at its wildest at this time of year with Odin riding his eight-legged horse Sleipnir across the sky. Children would leave their boots out filled with hay and sugar for Sleipnir on Winter Solstice Eve. In return Odin would leave them a gift for their kindness, very similar to nowadays with Father Christmas.

To the Norsemen celebrating Jol the central part of this three-day festival was the burning of a Yule log. The log was kept alight for three days during which people remembered their dead and believed that they too were sharing in the festival. A part of that tradition which has found its way into our own is our Yule logs except now they are made of chocolate and do not last as long!

It was a time of feasting, drinking, singing and recalling the ancient legends of Odin and Thor. On starry nights they would look to the sky where Odin might be travelling on Sleipnir. Sprigs of mistletoe were cut and evergreens were brought into the house. It is because of Odin's dominance over December that this month can be regarded as Odin's month. Whereas January can be interpreted as Thor's month and February can be seen as Freya's month.

For Wiccans and those who practices the Craft, Yule is a magical time and it is often associated with increasing magical powers. Alternative Christmas poems and stories come to the fore as ironically this time of year begins to be reclaimed by those original practioners of the old ways. Here is a poem of magic and wonder for young and old alike who celebrate Yule.

Twas the Night Before Yule

Twas the night before Yule, when all through the kingdom
Not a witch was stirring, not even the goblin
Who was very cruel, teasing the fairies with the salamander's tail.
All was quiet even the Banshee had silenced her wail;
While gremlins crept silently, stealing a Yule pie.
As a sleeping black cat raised one eye,

When up from the fire did the phoenix rise,

Startling the unicorn while pixies rubbed their eyes.

As out did crack from a giant egg of blue.

A baby dragon coughed, spluttered and flew.

Before setting the grand wizard's beard aglow.

As the High Priestess of the North weaved a spell of snow.

The elves jumped for joy at the thought of another toy,

For every girl and every boy.

All was good and all was bright, all on this Yule night.

The mermaids swam along Nessie.

While brownies cleaned as leprechauns wrapped a pressie.

The High Priestess of the frozen North.

Brings the freezing wind which jutters forth.

Her skin shines soft and fair and snow white is her hair.

As her sisters three make a merry change of seasons past,
present and future.

Spring, summer, autumn but she is always winter.

Her sister spring waits closely by.

She is carried by soft winds of March on high,

Or on the lion's roar.

While golden summer gives way to autumn's fall.

High Priestess of the South who governs spring.

Heralds all the wonder nature can bring.

She wields the fire and magic wands.

While her sister of summer rules water and ponds.

High Priestess of the West knows our hearts best.

For she is the Lady of the Lake.

As her sister of swords does summer take.

High Priestess of the East who governs Air.

Brings autumn's glow as she shakes her auburn hair.

Falling leaves crunch beneath the feet of Robin Goodfellow.

Ancient guardians of the secret vale.

Wax and wane in sun light and moon pale.

The great High Priestesses of seasons four work side by side.

As they love and teach what is good and right.

Each High Priestess governs the world we do not see,

Of fairies, leprechauns and pixies.

The world behind the veil hidden from you and me.

Yet all on this Midwinter's night.

Feel the magic in the Yule light.

We merry meet and merry part.

We all have magic in our hearts.

The Green Man did return and Merlin too,
Of all enchanted folk to view.
A magic Camelot and Avalon, waiting for the chosen one.
To pull the sword in the stone and free.
The genie that grants wishes of three.
A magic world on this magic night.
As the High Priestess whispers blessed be to all and to all a goodnight.

It is easy to see that the festivals of yesteryear have been caught up in our Christmas and Yule is no exception with vast quantities of food and feasting. However, while feasting we also remember the old and the lonely and those volunteers who go without their own festivities to provide meals for those less fortunate than ourselves. A basic principle of Norse philosophy is that if you receive a gift you must give something in return.

Here is a blessing for those who are less fortunate at this time of year.

Winter Healing Blessing

Light a blue candle for healing and keep it alight during your festivities. You could have it on the table during your meals to keep the flame of hope and love to others alive. Over the candle say these words:

> Blessed be to one and all.
> Those alone and without family.
> Father Odin help them through the festivity.
> Ease the pain of those suffering.
> Bring to them the warmth of spring.
> Father Odin thank you and blessed be.

As it is the festival period we have probably been with our families for a considerable amount of time. Although we love our families and there is much feasting. At times tempers can become frayed. If your family is at each other's throats then make this dessert. Being a witch is not all about potions and spells. We do make some fantastic food dishes too. Always record what you do in your book of shadows. Indeed in my family some members refer to the BOS as the 'recipe book.'

The Fruits of the North Baked Alaska Spell

The super berries from the frozen lands of northern climates lay dormant under the frozen land and bloom in spring then yield their fruits in autumn. These berries are highly nutritious such as blueberries, lingonberries and the beautiful named cloudberries. They are called super berries because they are high in anti-oxidants.

To make a Baked Alaska with blueberry ice-cream in the middle, first you need to make blueberry ice-cream.

There are many ways to make blueberry ice cream. The quick and easiest way is to get a tin of blueberries, drain and wash them. Then fold them into already made vanilla ice cream and put in freezer until you use it for the baked Alaska.

The other is to use fresh or frozen blueberries, double cream, milk, sugar, and egg yolks. You are basically going to make something called confectionary custard. With the sugar and milk try to limit them to either soya or low fat milk and try to use less sugar though some people can use up to 4 cups of sugar. Basically it is this: a pint of milk, a pint of cream and a pint of blueberries and 4 yolks.

Heat the milk, cream and half the sugar you want to use, up to 175 degrees. While doing that beat the egg yolks and remaining sugar up till it is a pale thick yellow colour. Then pour into the heated milk mixture and heat up to 180 degrees, do not boil. When it coats the back of a wooden spoon it is done. Then put it in an air tight container and leave to cool in the fridge. After take the custard out and put in a blender with the blueberries and blend everything. The berries should be broken down in the blender. Then put in the container and begin the freezing process. Unless you have an ice cream maker in which case follow the manufactures instructions. Otherwise it's the old way of making ice cream by taking it out of the freezer every 4 to 5 hours and blending or beating it up. You do this about three times before you can use it.

Experiment with making ice -cream it's actually quite fun thing to do, and if you have food intolerances you can try all different things to put in to flavour and make it creamy. You can put a vanilla pod or vanilla essence in the mixture also during the blending. See what you think as everyone's tastes are different.

Also try to limit your sugar and fat intake and just enjoy the fruit. We automatically reach for the sugar but nature has given us this super berry so try not to destroy it with a false sweetener like sugar. You could always use honey instead for a completely different type of taste.

Now you need to bring everything together to make the baked Alaska with the blueberry ice cream including the spell to bring a family together at festival time.

You need a sponge base, the blueberry ice cream, maybe some blueberry jam or mixed berry jam, egg whites and sugar.

Spread the mixed berry or blueberry jam on the sponge base and then place in the freezer. Preheat oven to 220C. Then whisk up 3 egg whites and 125g of sugar until it is stiff and forms peaks which do not move, this is now a good meringue mixture. Take out the base and ice cream out the freezer. As you scoop up a generous helping of the ice cream put it on the base while saying:

> Blessed family delight.
> Magic snow bright.
> Let my family treat each other right.
> To one and all blessed be.
> An it harm none so mote it be.

Then smother the ice cream and base in the egg white mixture, make sure everything is sealed in with the meringue. Then quickly put in the preheated oven for about 5 minutes or until the meringue starts to turn golden brown. Serve your magical dessert immediately to the family and see what happens.

The month of December is governed in the Zodiac by two signs; Sagittarius and Capricorn. Sagittarius can be found at the beginning of the month while Capricorn is the later finishing midway in January. Sagittarius is a fire sign while Capricorn is an earth sign. Yet both signs have strength within them and an air of noble loyalty to them. They would defend friends to the death and both despise any form of prejudice. These signs are in good company with their loyalty as December is the month governed by Odin.

Odin has over 200 names but it is as the 'Grey Wanderer,' we recognise him the most. Odin is referred to as the Grey Wanderer as he is said to wander the land in a grey hooded cloak. Some historians his image over the years has turned into Santa Claus. However, there are those that still like to believe that Father Odin still walks the land on cold winter nights making sure his flock are safe and protected.

Yet it is this image of the Grey Wanderer that artists and writers have been inspired by. We see the image of Odin in many places now. Gandalf the Grey from The Lord of the Rings Sagas is one such example.

Father Odin has many correspondences but one of them in particular is pine. There is a marvellous drink called Pine Nut drink and it is regarded by some as the champagne of the north. It is a sparkling spruce drink and is predominantly made in Finland. If you can, buy some for the Yuletide celebrations. Then raise a glass to Odin while saying Skal which implies a wish for good health and good fortune.

Charm of Odin

Create a good luck charm for the month of December with symbols of Odin. You will need some navy blue ribbon, some twigs from an ash tree, a pine cone and a symbol called the triquetra. If you can buy a charm of the triquetra that is much easier than drawing it as the triquetra is very difficult to draw and its strength lies in how it is drawn. The magical, protective nature of the triquetra is that it is drawn without the pen leaving the paper and consists of three interlocking triangles within a circle. It is very similar to the Valknut which is often referred to as the knot of Death and Rebirth.

However, we do not want the Valknut here, just the triquetra. It is a symbol of protection and the Turning of the Wheel. As it is also related to Odin we are asking Odin to protect all those in the house.

Tie the ash twigs, preferably three, together with the pine cone and triquetra with the navy blue ribbon. The ash twigs can be no more than 10cm in length. Please do not rip them from the tree; Odin would not be happy with that! Instead look on the ground around the ash tree the winter storms will have granted us what we need.

You can hang the charm up above your door or if you have a Christmas tree put the charm of Odin on it and see who notices. As you hang the charm say these words:

> Father Odin blessed be.
> Grant me a peaceful festivity.
> Let this house be full of love and harmony.
> Father Odin thank you and blessed be.

The ancestors used to make blessing water of the month. Basically, take a bowl of sea salt and leave in view of the full moon of that month. So if it is December it would be regarded as Odin's Blessing Water. Leave the bowl of sea salt in view of the full moon all night and in the morning take the salt and put it in an air tight container and tie a black or grey ribbon around it. This is Odin's salt and can be used for all manner of things but the main thing here is to make holy water or blessing water.

Odin Blessing Spray Spell

Fill a spray bottle with water and then put a tablespoon of Odin's salt in. Put 3 drops of pine essential oil in. Put the lid on the bottle and shake it up. Say these words as you do:

> Odin bless this spray.
> With your protection and strength.
> Keep evil far away.
> Keep me forever safe blessed be.
> An it harm none so mote it be.

Spray the water around when you feel you need extra protection either at home or at work. You can make as much or as less of the water as you need. Remember you will one use this water in the month of December.

A Midwinter Wedding

Winter months, winter fair.
Snow, frost, winter weather.
Blessed be,
Midwinter lovers everywhere.

A Midwinter wedding is a beautiful and magical affair. In Norse mythology the Trinity of Gods; Odin, Vili, and Ve made man and woman. Odin saw the trees Ash and Elm and gave them a new form; man and woman while Vili and Ve gave both the new forms souls and intelligence.

As such at a Midwinter wedding the Ash and Elm are present in some form either by young saplings of the trees which are planted by the couple to mark the occasion or by a twig of the trees placed on the tables of friends and family of the couple. For example, friends/family of the groom would have an Ash twig while friends/family of the bride has an elm twig.

You can also make gifts of wands from the trees. The bride's flowers such as garlands and bouquet can also have small twigs encased around the holly, Ivy and Hellebores or Christmas rose which makes a very pretty combination. Further, of course, do not forget mistletoe somewhere in the bride's flowers.

Performing a Midwinter Wedding

Handfasting is another name for a wedding. Handfasting is the joining together of two people or binding their souls together in this earth and for all lives. Therefore, it is something not to be taken lightly as there is no divorce in the Spirit world.

A Handfasting ceremony at any other time of the year would involve gold and silver cords. However, on this occasion we use green and silver for a Midwinter wedding. The green represents Freya who is the goddess of love. The silver cord is for Odin, as he is the Grey Wanderer. It is also Midwinter whose full moon is called the long night's moon.

The Handfasting is usually presided over by the High Priest/Priestess. The couple are expected to write their vows to one another. It is happy and loving occasion in which the witnesses can join in. This ceremony can be written out and given to the congregation to use, it is also a lovely keepsake when the day and Askr and Emblem's name is written on.

Here is an example of Midwinter Handfasting.

Ceremony

High Priest/Priestess
Blessed be to one and all.

All
Blessed Be

High Priest/Priestess
We are here today to join together Askr and Emblem. I ask Odin Father of all to bear witness to this union. I ask Freya to bless this union with love of these two souls forever. So mote it be.

All
So mote it be.

High Priest/Priestess
Askr and Emblem whose mortal names are .... (Bride's name) and ....(groom's name). Do you join us here of your own free will this Midwinter?

Bride/Groom

I do.

High Priest/Priestess

Then I ask you to now speak your vows in the presence of Odin and Freya. As your family and friends bear witness to your union.

Bride/Groom (Speak their vows to each other.)

High Priest/Priestess

AS I bind their hands with these cords it reminds us that we are forever joined. Though the cord is not tied as we are also free to grow and support each other with love. In the name of love. In the name of Freya. So mote it be.

All

So mote it be.

High Priest/Priestess

Now (groom's name) and (bride's name) say your oath together.

Bride/Groom

Heart and mind to thee.
Body and soul to thee.
I love and protect thee.
Forever so mote it be.

High Priest/Priestess

We have now witnessed the joining of Askr and Emblem together in love and matrimony. I give thanks to great Odin and blessed Freya for their presence. Blessed be.

All

Blessed be.

High Priest/Priestess

I now pronounce (bride's name) and (groom's name) husband and wife. Blessed be.

All

Blessed be.

Wedding Feast

A Midwinter feast can also be used as a Midwinter wedding feast. The drinks can be a mulled wine punch. While a non-alcoholic version can be made with red grape juice, though add water to this as it can be very sweet.

A typical midwinter feast would have lots of meat and fish dishes with hardy root vegetables such as turnips, potatoes and swedes in. Therefore, a stew, casserole, dumplings, roasts meats such as beef, pork and also pheasants, duck and game can be served. If however you are vegan then there are still many choices. A good saying to remember is:

'There is a salad for every season.'

A winter salad can include cabbage, chicory and celery. Any cooked vegetable such as beetroot, carrots, cauliflower, swedes and turnips can all make an interesting and nutritional rich salad when cubed and mixed with nuts like walnuts and raisins then tossed in olive oil and Worcestershire sauce.

Also do not forget about herbs. A salad of parsley, chick peas, tomatoes and beetroot is delicious. As is mint, spinach and diary free yogurt all mashed together. Hummus and couscous are perfect too with roasted sweet potato, parsnip and carrot wedges used as dips. Breads made with peppers, saffron, pumpkin seeds are also perfect to eat. Along with stuffed mushrooms and peppers are also hearty dishes for a feast.

Desserts can be anything from mini lemon cheesecakes to syllabubs made with whisky and berries, or banana layer cake made with butterscotch and pecans.

Wedding Menu

Starters

Mulligatawny Soup

Winter Salad

Royal Soup

Main

Whisky and Cranberry Glazed Goose

Baked Cauliflower

Potato Ribbons

Creamed Swede and Carrot with Nutmeg

Cranberry Sauce

Vegetarian: Winter Risotto or Vegetable Goose

Dessert

Winter Mess (apples with meringue)

Snow Pudding

Freya's Rhubarb and Banana Amber

Drinks

Mulled Wine

Mulled Wine (non-alcoholic made with red grape juice)

Sweets

Coffee

Midwinter Tea

Freya's Chocolate Whisky Fondue

Wedding Recipes

Here are some of the lesser-known recipes of the Midwinter Wedding Feast.

Winter Salad

A winter salad is very easy to make. Decide the quantity needed and add ingredients accordingly. Here is the basic recipe for winter salad.

1 Stick celery
1 cooked beetroot
4 cooked potatoes
1 tablespoon of chopped parsley
Salt and pepper
Salad dressing - olive oil and Worcestershire sauce.

There are two ways to make a winter salad. Traditionally slice the vegetables and shred the celery. Then arrange vegetables in separate layers before adding the salt and pepper. Then cover with salad dressing.

The other way is to slice and dice all vegetables including celery. Place all in a large bowl add salt and pepper, and pour the salad dressing in and toss all ingredients together. You can add chopped walnuts and raisins if desired. A handful of cranberries make a nice midwinter tradition. The other addition can be raw Brussels sprouts which can be sliced and added to the dish instead of celery. Cooked chestnuts are also a good replacement for walnuts.

Royal Soup

The Royal Soup is a basic clear soup with egg and milk added. Clear soup is anything but clear. It is made with brown stock, beef, carrots, onion, celery, peppercorns, allspice, and cloves. So a lovely winter soup though it can be used any time of the year.

Vegetable Goose

The Vegetable Goose is actually quite easy to make. Basically it is bread which has been soaked in cold water, 1 onion, 1 tablespoon chopped sage, butter, pepper and salt, and chopped walnuts.

Squeeze bread nearly dry and mash it up along with all the other ingredients chopped small. The bake in a hot oven for about 30 - 45 mins. Serve with the other vegetable dishes on the menu and the cranberry sauce.

Desserts

The Snow Pudding is actually a lemon sponge with custard poured over it.

Winter Mess is basically the winter version of Eton Mess just made with apples instead of strawberries. The apples can be cooked then mixed with double cream and crushed meringue. Cinnamon is nice winter addition to this dish also. You could also make it with vanilla custard with sprinkle of nutmeg. Make sure you crush the meringue into the custard and do not have the custard too hot as the meringue could melt into it.

Freya's Rhubarb and Banana Amber

This does not involve eating the stone amber; it just refers to the topping of the pudding. Freya's Rhubarb and Banana Amber can be a bit fussy to make but once made is a welcome treat. Amber is also the stone of Freya our Norse goddess of love.

This is what you need:

2 bundles of rhubarb
4 bananas
50g of castor sugar
50g of mixed cake crumbs
2 eggs
2 finely crushed macaroons

Wash and cut the rhubarb into inch length. Peel and slice bananas then using a small amount of water a sugar stew them both together until tender. Then place in a blender for about two mins. After stir in the cake crumbs and egg yolks and put mixture in a buttered pie dish and bake in a moderately warm oven for about 20 mins. While that is baking whisk the egg

whites until stiff and fold the sugar in. After the oven mixture is done cover roughly with the egg white. Then sprinkle the crushed macaroons over it. Return to oven for another 10 - 15mins until the surface is golden brown like amber.
Serve this dish either hot or cold.

This can be made with gooseberries. Yet as it's for a wedding bananas and rhubarb are quite appropriate, as they are both regarded as aphrodisiacs.

Another great aphrodisiac is of course chocolate. This last dish is a lovely treat any time of the year and rounds an evening off perfectly.

Freya's Chocolate Whisky Fondue

Cooking chocolate
Thick double cream
Whisky
Fruit cut into wedges (nectarines, peaches, cherries)

Melt the chocolate over a double boiler. Then remove from heat. Fold in 2 tablespoons of double cream. Then gently stir in 4 tablespoons of whisky. Place fruit wedges on wooden toothpicks and allow people to eat and dip at their leisure. The whisky enhances the flavour of the fruit.

Midwinter Tea

Midwinter tea is a mixture of black or green tea with orange peel, cloves, almond pieces, chopped walnuts, and cranberry. Hot water is poured over the mixture and allowed to brew for about 5 minutes before serving hot. Try to avoid an artificial sweetener and use either a slice of lemon or a slice of orange for a complete winter feel.

January

'A January spring is worth nothing.'

Our weather can play tricks on us and a warm mild January is a worry. It is precisely like the saying a warm January actually means nothing. Furthermore, January is the middle of winter it is the month where we expect terrible weather. We expect snows and bitter frosts which are helpful to us and the environment as they kill germs and bacteria. This delightful saying from 17th century England brings the point home:

'A green winter makes a full churchyard'

As a mild winter makes germs and bacteria multiply. So when the biting wind is making your teeth judder just remember the freezing temperatures are having a good effect. Indeed the coldest day of the year is traditionally January 13th or 14th. It was in January that the Thames froze as did ale and wine so much so people began to sell them in weight rather than volume. Yet the coldest day of the year usually coincides with

St. Hilary and both the 13th and 14th of January have been used as the saint's day.

January is named after the Roman God Janus. He is a two faced God with one face looking back and the other looking forward. So he is a perfect God to ask for help if you are trying to make plans or heal a rift with its origins in the past.

Forgive Myself Spell

The winter is often a time of reflection. We think of things that happened in the past. We think of the present. We begin to make plans for the future either for summer holidays or planning for the future with a short or long term plan. Use this snow spell for developing your plans. It will put you in the right frame of mind to make changes in your life.

This is a forgiveness spell. Sometimes we may have done things in the past that we are not happy with or we feel we could have done better. We may have handled a situation better or we may have said something to someone that we instantly regret. In order to move on and make plans for the future we have to let go of the past and forgive ourselves. Use the power of the pure white snow to move on.

This is a two-part spell. First we must let go of the past and move on then we need to focus on the future and what we need to do in order to achieve the life we want.

Light a white candle and look out of the window as you say this spell:

> Sprinkle Sprinkle little flakes.
> In my life I have made mistakes.
> Sprinkle Sprinkle forgiving snows.
> Please wipe clean all my woes.
> Things I have said I now regret.
> Things I have done.
> I ask forgiveness of me.
> An it harm none.
> So mote it be.

After you have said the spell meditate and think of things you have done, no matter how painful. Imagine the light of the flame illuminating your past sending negative thoughts away.

After you have meditated for a while keep the candle burning and turn your mind to the future. What do you want the future to be? Make a plan about where you see yourself in one year, in two years, three years and then onto five years. Give yourself achievable targets in each year.

To help you visualise and break down your goal. You can use the chart of manifestation and go on to write out your plans and follow the rest of the spell. You can download the colour chart of manifestation in the reader's area when you register your copy of this book at www.seasonsspellsandmagic.com

The Process

Write out your plans on white paper with a blue pen. Title the paper 'My Goal for One Year.' Then on a separate piece of paper for each write, 'My Goal for Two Years, My Goal for Three Years,' and so on. This spell is a good long spell. Do not try to rush doing it. This spell and the casting of the spell should take at least two to three hours. After place your plans in front of you and say:

> Sprinkle sprinkle little snow.
> How far I will go.
> Sprinkle sprinkle little snow might.
> Let my future be forever bright.
> Let my plans come to pass.
> My future is right at last.
> A good happy future for me.
> An it harm none so mote it be.

Fold the papers your future plans are on, one way for the 1st year page, two ways for the 2nd year page, and three ways for the third year and so on. Then keep out of sight of prying eyes in a place that you can easily see every day. Occasionally throughout the year take out your year one plan and look at it. See where you are with your goals.

Then to the day you cast your spell take out your year one plan and look at it. Give thanks to that which you have accomplished. Light a white candle and while giving thanks burn your year one plan and bury the ashes in the garden.

The art of fortune telling and divination is traditional at several points throughout the year but none more so than at New Year. In Victorian times New Year's Eve was a mixture of divination parties with all manner of items from playing cards to dropping melted wax in cold water to see the initial of a future husband or wife. Phrenology was extremely popular parlour game during this time as it told of a person's character and subsequent future simple by feeling the bumps on a person's head. However, January is one if the main times of the year that fortune telling was expected. As in this season we are looking at the north one of the main forms of divination is the north was the runes. The runes are an extremely difficult form of divination.

Divination by Runes

The runes as we know them are about two thousand years old. However, many of the symbols themselves are much older. The runes were a form of an alphabet and were carved on stone or wood. The actual word rune is linked with the Norse word for 'mystery' or 'secret.'

There are a number of different rune alphabets which have anything from 14 to 33 characters. Today our most common runic packs come in 24. Once you understand what the meanings are it becomes easier to read the runes.

The Runes

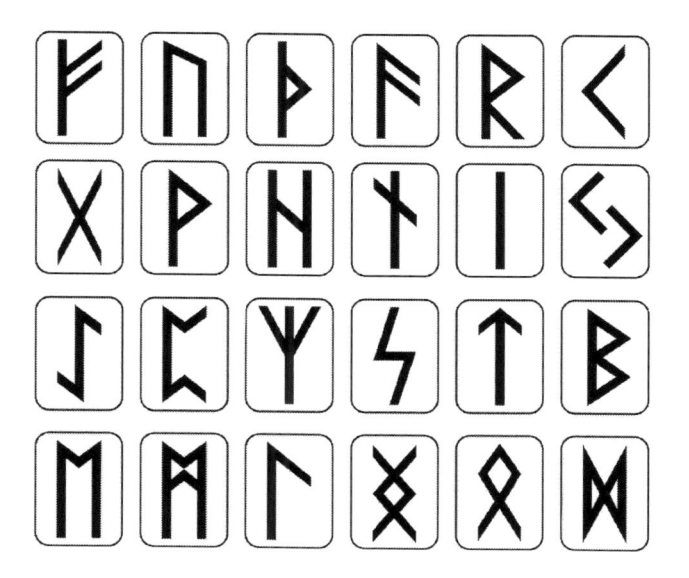

Here are the runes English meanings:

Feoh - F - Cattle

Think about it if you had cattle then you would have had wealth so the appearance of Feoh means income, wealth, prosperity, status and power.

Ur - U - Wild Ox

What does an ox mean? The ox is a strong beast and works hard therefore the appearance of Ur in a reading means strength, raw power, and a chance to prove yourself. However it can also mean a sudden change.

Thorn - Th - A thorn

Think about what a thorn is therefore its meaning in a reading means double-edged luck. Yet it can also mean protection albeit physical, mental and spiritual.

Ansur - A - A god

Think of what a god means and in the Norse pantheon the Head of the Gods is Odin. Therefore, in a reading Ansur means authority, divine force, wisdom, knowledge and communication.

Rad - R - A wheel

Think what a wheel is and therefore its meaning in a reading is that of movement. A journey which includes spiritual, it also means exploration and progress.

Ken - K - A bonfire

Think what a fire meant to our ancestors; illumination, the primal fire. It also means creativity and health but it also signifies a new love.

Geofu - G - A gift

The gift means precisely that giving and receiving, it is an opportunity and also talent. Yet it also means partnership or a union.

Wyn - W - Joy

The appearance of this means precisely that of joy, happiness, success and winning. However, it can also mean peace, creative work and travel.

Hagal - H - Hail

This means the completely unexpected or a disruptive sudden event. If we compare this rune to the tarot it has similar meanings to the Tower.

Nyd - N - Need

This represents all our needs such as shelter, food, warmth, security and also safety.

Is - I - Ice

Think about ice and what it does. Thus we find the meaning of this rune. It means the freezing of movement or action; it is a pause or delay, stagnation in plans.

Ger - J - Season

The meaning of this card is precisely that the cycle of the year. Therefore, harvest, fruits of hard work, conclusion, justice, a favourable outcome to your endeavours.

Yr - Y - Yew tree

The yew tree is symbolic of death and rebirth. Therefore, in addition to that this rune also means protection, defence but also of struggle.

Peorth - P - A dice cup

This means fate, game of life, disclosure or a secret.

Eolh - Z - Hand Greeting
This means friendship of course but also protection and healing.

Sigel - S - Sun
Think about what the sum means to us: success. Therefore, in a reading this means victory, clear vision and brilliance.

Tyr - T - The war god
Yes, this rune does mean combat albeit physical, emotional or spiritual. However, this rune also means justice and courage.

Beorc - B - Birch tree
The meaning of this rune is fertility and regeneration. Yet it also means the home, purification and new beginnings.

Eoh - E - A horse
Travel of course. Yet it also means a partnership or marriage, trust, change and/or adjustment.

Man - M - Human/People

Therefore, the appearance of this rune in a reading means the human experience, co-operation, sharing and assistance.

Lagu - L - Water

This rune refers to the spiritual element or intuition. It also means imagination, flowing movement. However, water is also synonymous with love and therefore the appearance of this rune means love.

Ing - Ng - The God Ing

This rune is symbolic of male sexuality, energy and protection of the home.

Daeg - D - Day

The day means 'new start,' or light albeit divine light. It can also mean a change of heart or growth.

Odal - O - Home

This rune means belonging, the family, the property or the land itself.

There is also a new addition to many sets of runes it is a blank rune called the **Wyrd**. The Wyrd means karma. It is one of those symbols that if it appears in a reading then it counteracts all the other runes. It also means that the particular question should not be pursued. However, if you should purchase a set of runes and find a blank rune or the Wyrd in the set then you can always cast it aside as the concept of destiny is already covered by the Peorth rune.

In the beginning it helps if you handle or charge the runes as much as possible of your energy. You can keep them in a cloth bag and also sleep with them under your pillow. Then when you cast the runes try to use a flat surface and place a white cloth down. It would be advised to ask for the protection and guidance of Odin or another Norse God or Goddess you have a particular kin to. Learn the runes and have fun using them but always be respectful.

Spells and Charms

The full moon in January is the festival of Thurseblot or Thor's feast. The Norse God of lightening who is protector of Midgard which is earth. At this festival Thor is invoked to drive back the frost giant Jotun himself, not quite as cute as our Jack Frost. So that spring may return to the earth.

If you have a battle coming up or you need to fight for yourself in the work environment call upon the force of Thor. Light a red candle on a Thursday and say this spell:

Battle Ahead Spell

> Mighty Thor big and strong.
> Help me fight the negative one.
> Grant me victory in the battle ahead.
> Mighty Thor grant me success.
> Let me be simply the best.
> Mighty Thor blessed be.
> An it harm none so mote it be.

Imagine yourself victorious and holding up your prize.

Charm of Thor

Further as January is the month of Thor then create a charm of Thor to hang in the house all this long month. You will need red ribbon, three twigs from an oak tree, some acorns, and a charm of Thor's hammer. The acorns if you like can be sprayed silver or gold to match the charm. Though leaving everything natural gives a rustic touch to it all. Tie the twigs, acorns and charm of Thor's hammer with the red ribbon and hang in the kitchen or up above the door. Once again please do not pull the twigs from the tree or the acorns from the tree, nature will have granted us what we need so please look on the ground. The twigs only need to be 10cm in length. As you hang the charm say these words:

> Blessed Thor protect all in this house.
> None shall enter who brings harm.
> Mighty Thor please protect me.
> Mighty Thor blessed be.

January is probably one of the most depressing months of the year. It has none of the joyful festivals that December has. It has also none of the forthcoming spring festivals like February. In January the days can still be long. Sometimes the sun seems to disappear for days even weeks in January. This has led some to calculate that the most depressing day of the year is in mid to late January which is anywhere from 17th to 25th January. Interestingly, the happiest day of the year is in June close to the Midsummer Solstice.

However, the most depressing day of the year is often referred to as Blue Monday. Counteract this negativity and darkness with this 'lift my spirit' spell. On Blue Monday or anytime in January when you feel depressed cast this spell.

Place a yellow candle, orange candle, and a red candle in a triangle. Light them and with your hands open with palms turned up to the universe say these words:

Lift My Spirit Spell

> Light chase the darkness away.
> Free me from the blues today.
> No more the winter sadness.
> No more the winter chill.
> Take away your woe and ills.
> I embrace the light.
> I embrace the day.
> No more this eternal night.
> From depression let me be free.
> An it harm none so mote it be.

Keep the candles burning as long as you can and embrace their light. Embrace the illumination of the candles lighting up the corners of darkness in your life.

The depression of January is not helped by the lack of natural life in gardens and parks. Yet look beyond the emptiness and you will see how full of life everything actually is. The trees though they look dead are far from it and the spirits within the trees are still wide awake.

It is in January that we have many customs and festivals regarding our trees.

On 17th January people in a little village in Somerset, England go to one of the orchards and make a circle around one of the largest apple trees. They decorate the tree in toast which has been soaked in cider. They also pour cider over the tree. Guns are fired into the branches and a song is sung to the tree. This ensures the tree will have a good crop of apples in the coming year. This very old ceremony is called Wassailing the Apple Trees. It was intended to do two things. It scared away the evil spirits with the guns and it was also an offering to the spirits of the tree itself.

We believe that there are spirits in trees. They are good spirits and not just the Will-o'-the-wisps of yore. Incidentally there are magical spells in the autumn section of this book all about will-o'-the-wisps as seeing these curious little tree spirits in autumn are indicators of where buried treasure is hidden. They are most indeed good little sprites.

Nevertheless, the spirits of the trees would grant people good harvests and help them to have children. Indeed, groves of trees led many people to places of worship thus trees formed the first temples. Many cultures around the world set up festivals around trees. Indeed, Native Americans set up a cottonwood tree at the centre of their summer festivals. Let us therefore ask for the help of tree spirits even in the depths of winter.

Tree Spirits in Celtic mythology are used instead of the zodiac we have the tree signs of when people are born. You can see the list of tree signs on the next page

Tree Signs

Reed - October 28th - November 23rd
Elder - November 24th - December 23rd
Birch - December 24th - January 20th
Rowan - January 21st - February 17th
Ash - February 18th - March 17th
Alder - March 18th - April 14th
Willow - April 15th - May 12th

Hawthorn - May 13th - June 9th
Oak - June 10th - July 7th
Holly - July 8th - August 4th
Hazel - August 5th - September 1st
Vine - September 2nd - September 29th
Ivy - September 30th - October 27th

Trees are also amazing healers. We can learn so much from them. Just look at the willow, it gives us the humble aspirin. Every year we are learning new things about the aspirin with doctors now advising us to take a daily dose of it.

In the Scandinavian forests of Finland people have long since known of the healing effects of Birch sap. The sap contains proteins, amino acids and enzymes not to mention sugar of course. It is used as a tonic in the traditional herbal medicine of Finland and also Russia.

Further let us not forget about Maple Syrup. Compared to other sweeteners such as honey, it has at least 15 more times calcium in it. Scientists are also finding health benefits of maple syrup believing it contains anti-oxidants. Yet healers have known about these benefits for years, and let us not forget that we were termed as healers first before we were called witches.

Embrace the strength of trees and make a maple syrup elixir for ourselves. However, if you can find some Finnish Birch sap then use that instead.

Tree Spirit Spell

Boil the kettle and when the water is boiled pour into a cup. Taking the syrup put a tablespoon of either maple syrup or birch sap into the boiling water. Gently stir clockwise while saying:

> Gods of the north, hear me please.
> Let that which I lack.
> Now begin to attract.
> Strong and healthy like the mighty tree.
> Let my strength return to me.
> An it harm none so mote it be.

Then slowly sip your tree water and imagine yourself gaining the strength as if from the earth. Let the strength creep up you beginning in your feet to your legs and up your body. You stand firm and strong bending in the breeze, able to withstand all. Blessed be.

There are many magical occurrences that happen in the winter and it just does not concern the magic of snow or Jack Frost. The Northern Lights are a wondrous sight to behold and always worth a visit. They are predominately seen in the winter months. There are many legends connected with the Aurora Borealis. One of them is that they signify a new generation coming to the earth. How strange that the solar flare became the best light show of the past 50 years would coincide with the 2012 winter solstice and the new turning of the world. The children born now after 2012 are here for a reason, a new enlightened generation.

The Aurora Borealis or the Northern Lights stream across a cold night sky and look for all intents and purposes like angel's wings fluttering across the sky. They are simply beautiful and a sight worth seeing

Northern Lights Spell

Try to have a picture of the Aurora Borealis. Incidentally there is a wondrous picture taken at the Giant's Causeway in Northern Ireland. It was taken in 2012 and is simply awe inspiring. The Giant's Causeway is magical on any day. The ancestors are around constantly there. Yet on a particular evening in April 2012 saw a very rare event, the Northern Lights dancing over the Giant's Causeway.

Magic is all around us and at times can amaze even those who work with it on a daily basis. Yet these pictures of the Northern Lights over the Giant's Causeway are further proof that magic is there for all to see and work with.

So even if you never see the Northern Lights where you live. Go outside if you can on a moonlit cloudless winter night sky. Look up at the stars and cast a spell of healing to a friend in need.

> Blessed be to the night sky.
> Dancing lights of centuries past.

Grant me a wish at last.

My friend (name) is suffering.

On medicines she/he relies.

Dancing Northern Lights of the night skies.

Send your magic healing blessed be.

An it harm none so mote it be.

> 'Winter's thunder makes summer wonder.'

This is great saying on a magnificent wonder of nature. It is truly a rare event and one in which we can work quite a bit of magic from due to its unique origin. A thunderstorm in winter which accompanies a snow storm is a blessing from Thor. Thundersnow is excellent to collect for snow spells and to witness the lightening through a snowstorm is also amazing to watch as it looks very similar to a show of the Northern Lights. It is a rare event but those who live south of the Northern Lights who may never see them, a Thundersnow storm can be called poor man's Aurora Borealis.

Collect as much of the Thundersnow as possible and keep it labelled in the freezer. Use it for your snow spells but use sparingly as it is such a rare event.

Thor's Blessing Water

This is similar to Odin's Blessing Water of December it is made the same way. Except in January and with a red ribbon tied around the jar of sea salt. Remember to charge your sea salt with the full moon of January which corresponds to Thor's Feast so it is perfect to make the salt with. Also with Thor we use 3 drops of Juniper essential oil in the spray bottle with the water. While shaking it up say:

> Mighty Thor bestow your strength upon me.
> Great Thor scatter my enemies.
> Keep those who would do harm far away from me.
> Though it harm none so mote it be.

Remember use this only in the month of January. You can use this at home or at work if you feel like there is enemy around you.

January in the Zodiac is month which governed by both the strength and loyalty of the Capricorn and the realm of ideas and possibility that is the air sign of Aquarius. Aquarius is the sign of the abstract thinker. The earth goes through ages each age lasts 2150 years and we have just left the age of Pisces. Think what those two millennia brought us. We have now moved into the Age of Aquarius. It is interesting to think what wonders Aquarius will bring as we already know this is the sign of the abstract thinker.

February

'If in February there be no rain,
The hay won't goody, nor the grain.'

It is essential it rains or snows in February, if it does not then the rivers and reservoirs will be empty and in the summer there will bring a drought. Winter rain and snow is paramount to a healthy and good harvest. If we have dry mild winters we have summer droughts. So it is very important the wet weather is in the winter months and as February is the last of the winter month's farmers and gardeners watch this month eagerly.

One of the most charming festivals of all is found in the cold month of February; Imbolc. The month of February is often viewed as the month of Freya. Many of the festivals in February focus on that which Freya governs. The Goddess Freya is responsible for love, beauty, fertility, gold, war and death. She is responsible for collecting the souls of soldiers and warriors and taking them to Valhalla. So she is a very important deity to be aware of.

In February the delightful festival of Imbolc gives us hope and renews our strength. Translated it literally means in the belly and it is at this time the quickening begins. The earth begins to burst with life once again. The sweetness of spring is beginning to envelop us again. Imbolc coincides with Candlemas on the 2nd February. There are many sayings concerned with Candlemas which help to predict the coming of winter:

> 'If Candlemas Day be fair and bright,
> Winter will have another fight.
> But if Candlemas Day be clouds and rain,
> Winter is gone and will not come again.'

This is a bit similar to the American custom of Groundhog Day, that if a groundhog sees his shadow on 2nd February then there will be another six weeks of winter. Yet despite its ferocity February is a sweet month with many festivals and happy celebrations in.

Spells and Charms

Here is a spell to make Imbolc sweets which are hard boiled sweets. They are made with the fruits of the north. The fruits of the north contain many health benefits. Although blueberry is readily available, try to make some hard boiled sweets out of other fruits of Scandinavia such as cloudberries and lingonberries. These berries grow wild and in abundance in the great forests of Finland. Here for Imbolc we shall make blueberry hard boiled candy.

Imbolc Blueberry Sweet Spell

You will need a cooking thermometer, caster sugar, golden syrup, some water and a handful of blueberries. When you begin to make your own candy and sweets you will come to realise how much sugar actually goes into sweets that we buy. It comes as no surprise the numbers of people developing diabetes in our modern day and age. Start with this recipe but then try to experiment and limit the amount of sugar used. The key to always getting candy and fudge to set is the right temperature so invest in a good cooking thermometer.

450g caster sugar
250g golden syrup
2-3 tablespoons water
10 - 20 blueberries

Put all ingredients in saucepan and stir just as sugar dissolves then do not stir again as it creates air bubbles and your candy will not set. Bring to the boil and heat up to 155 degrees C. Also drop a small amount of the mixture into cold water and see if it forms hard brittle threads, if it does the mixture is ready.

After, pour into a tray lined with greased proof paper. Then let it cool and after about 20 - 30 minutes begin to cut small pieces off and shape into little balls. Then roll in icing sugar to serve or to keep. The icing sugar stops the sweets from sticking together. You can experiment with this recipe. Blueberries are very strong in flavour and in colour so start with only 10 in the mixture and boil them all up with the sugar and syrup.

While you are rolling them up into little balls in the icing sugar say this spell.

Sweet and warm.

Tender and juicy.

Bring summer happiness to me.

No more the winter chills.

Frozen hands and rosy cheeks.

Sweet and warm.

Tender and juicy.

Bring the summer happiness,

Back to me.

An it harm none so mote it be.

Pop the sweet in your mouth and let the flavours trigger your memories of summer. Imagine the warmth, the bees humming and the flowers and trees in full bloom.

Some recipes of hard candy call for artificial colours and sweeteners but try to limit the colours and just use natural products like the fruit itself. You can use this recipe and explore different flavours with fruits, herbs and spices. Always record everything in your Grimoire, or 'recipe' book, even your failures. We learn from our mistakes, spells and magic are no different.

Vanadanite Charm Necklace

Vanadis is one of Freya's many names and is the root source for the chemical compound extract vanadium. This is because of its many coloured compounds. From vanadis we get the crystal Vanadanite. Try to have a necklace made of it or find a piece of it and keep it in the bedroom. Vanadanite can be called the passion stone or the sex stone. It is a stone of the sacral chakra where sexuality lies. As Freya is also known as the Goddess of Sex this stone is often associated with her. Freya is strong and forceful and goes after whatever or whoever she desires.

We are going to create a Vanadanite charm necklace or if not a necklace then a piece of Vanadanite. Keep the piece by the bed. On a Friday say these words over your Vanadanite.

> Bless this night.
> Love that feels so right.
> Let me have the passion tonight.
> Goddess Freya bless this Vanadanite.

Freya's Magic Massage Oil

'To St. Valentine the spring is a neighbour.'

As Valentine's Day also falls in February combine Freya and Valentine for passion. Use Freya's Magic Massage oil for sensual sexual nights. Create some massage oil with amber oil and peach oil. Use the base or carrier oil of sweet almond oil.

6 drops of amber essential oil
6 drops of peach essential oil
25ml of sweet almond oil

Put all ingredients in a dark bottle and shake up. As you shake it up say these words:

Bring together my love and me.
Let us embrace our sexuality.
Let us have a night to remember.
Let this night bring us closer together.
Blessed Freya thank you for giving love to me.
An it harm none so mote it be.

Then date and label it Freya's Magic Massage Oil. This oil will last about 6 months.

One other item you can make as it is Valentine's Day, or Freya's love day is making Freya Love Biscuits. The recipe has ingredients that are sacred to love itself, the passion and the warmth and also sacred to Freya.

Freya Love Biscuits

100g of flour
100g of butter
50g of sugar
1 egg yolk
The rind of half a lemon
1/2 teaspoon of baking powder
1/2 teaspoon of saffron
50g of chopped cherries

Cream butter and sugar together then add lemon rind, chopped cherries and beat in yolk. Add flour, baking powder, saffron and mix all together. Roll out and cut with a heart shaped cutter. Bake in a hot oven (425f/220c) for 15 - 20 minutes. Take out then leave to cool and enjoy. You could indulge further by dipping half the heart biscuit in melted chocolate and leave to set before enjoying.

Saffron and cherries are perfect companions for love spells, equal amounts of passion and love are an excellent combination.

February is a magical month as any month is but there is definitely something extra about February, especially in a Leap Year. There are many traditions with a leap year and one of them is that a woman can propose to a man on that day. The 29th February comes around every four years, so women do have to wait a while to propose. However, if the man refuses tradition states that he must by the poor lady twelve pairs of gloves to hide her shame of not having a wedding ring!

Furthermore, bad luck is also said to be evident on that day of course. In Scotland it is considered bad luck if someone is born on the 29th February. In Greece however it is bad luck for couples to marry at all in a leap year and it is especially unlucky on the actual leap day.

However, as it is the 29th February the spring is certainly on its way and the warmth is coming. Here is a leap year spell to embrace the sunshine.

Leap Year Spell

> Leap frog, leap year.
> Leaping lords, shed no tears.
> Let sadness leap from me.
> Let sunshine leap to me.
> Leap frog, leap year.
> An it harm none so mote it be.

Winter is often a time of quiet contemplation but in the month of February beauty takes hold. The month of February although still winter can be a time of preparing for the spring and the coming summer. Use the time for beauty treatments in the winter and prepare your legs and feet for shorts and sandals. Create your own spa in the bathroom. Call upon Freya the Goddess of beauty to help you.

There are a number of beauty products you can make at this time of year. Fill a clean old sock with rolled oats tie onto the tap while you are running your bath. If you put 4 drops of amber essential oil in the sock with the oats you have created Freya's Sensual Bath. Let the tap water run through the sock creating a soft warm luxurious bath. You can light candles and soak in the soft water and make sure you are not disturbed.

Furthermore, make hair rinse using homemade vinegar. Making vinegar can be a bit of work and you need to be patient but once made you will never go back to bought vinegars. Apples are also sacred to Freya so February is a perfect time to make vinegar.

You will need at least 12 apples thoroughly washed. Any type of apple is good for making vinegar so experiment with different types as they all have suitable tastes. Then peel and core the apples, you can use the flesh of the apples for anything you want. Perhaps you could make an apple crumble with the flesh. While the core and peel is all you need for vinegar.

Put the peel and cores in a wide-mouthed crock and cover with water. Put the lid on and leave in a warm place to ferment. Taste the liquid every few days and stir occasionally. Take the froth off the vinegar as the vinegar starts to ferment. The taste of the vinegar will develop depending on the temperature. When you have the taste you want then strain the vinegar into a large bowl. Clean the crock but do not use detergent or soap on it. After pour the vinegar into a bottle, label and date it. The bottled vinegar will clear if it is cloudy.

You can always return a small amount of the vinegar to the crock to become the vinegar 'mother' of future vinegars but do this only if you intend to keep making vinegar.

To make vinegar hair rinse use 250ml/1 cup of water to 1 tablespoon of herbal vinegar. Add the herbs into the vinegars in the bottle pertaining to what you need. Use sage vinegar to darken hair and chamomile and lemon to lighten hair or if your hair is blond. Parsley vinegar is good to cure dandruff while rosemary vinegar is good to condition dry or thinning hair.

Charm of Freya

As February is the month of Freya we can make a charm for her. Freya's correspondences among others are the alder, apple, mint, rose, feathers and of course amber or Vanadanite. However for this charm we will use three twigs 10cm in length from the apple tree, some sprigs of mint, a red rose and a feather. Tie all these up in a pretty bundle with green ribbon and hang either in your bedroom or bathroom. As you do say these words:

> Goddess Freya blessed be.
> Please bring your gifts to me.
> Let love, passion and beauty.
> In this home wander free.
> An it harm none so mote it be.

Keep your charms from year to year or make new ones. You can always make them as little gifts to likeminded friends for birthday presents among other things. You can make a basket up of a charm, a spell or blessing, and some handmade sweets as a gift to someone. Always write down your gift baskets in your BOS so you can remember what you gave to people each year.

Freya's Blessing Water

This is made similar to Odin and Thor's Holy Water, with sea salt, and water. However, as this is Freya's Blessing Water it is on February's full moon. Also for Freya's Blessing Water use 3 drops of rose essential oil. This water is perfect holy water for blessing the area and yourself for love. While shaking up the blessing water say these words to ask Freya for help:

> Goddess Freya please bestow your gifts.
> Love, passion and desire come to me.
> Let love be present in every room.
> Let my desires come to be.
> An it harm none so mote it be.

February is the month of Freya and love. In the Zodiac then it is no surprise that we find Aquarius and the sign of unconditional self-sacrificing love which is Pisces. Pisces is the sign of the fishes; perfection and procrastination. Pisces is also the sign of Spirit, the sixth sense that resides in us all. In this sign it is the most prominent. As such, during the time of Pisces from February 19th to 20th March many people may experience psychic phenomena more than any other part of the year. Yet do not fear it and work with the energy if you so wish. If you choose not to then merely tell the energy, or however, the psychic phenomena has manifested to leave.

The charms of winter are endless. The many variants of the weather help us to construct spells and magical work alongside these differences. Snow, ice, Thundersnow and dark days all help and guide us to develop our magic. The spells and practices of yesteryear are still used. Yet they continue to develop alongside our modern lives. Magic and the Craft grows as we grow. By honouring and acknowledging our ancestors' words and beliefs we continue to develop. The one thing we must always remember is the Rede:

An it harm none, do what ye wilt.

Therefore, try the many different spells in this season and work alongside nature. Always remember to record your magic work as your BOS, Book of Shadows, can be passed onto future generations who can also add their own magic work to it. In the next chapter we will look at the season of spring and the wondrous festivals, weather and Gods it holds.

Blessed Be

Conclusion: The Seasonal Witch

The passing seasons that make the year of our earth are blessings. They give us the fruits and berries, the warmth of the sun, and the joy of the spring, even in winter with harsh barren cold that brings frosts and snows has a purpose. The purpose is to rest and renew. So much of our lives nowadays are as full in winter as they are in summer. Yet all beings need rest at some point during the year and not just two vacations with family and friends.

The magic and spell that accompany the seasons help us to connect with that part of us which has disappeared from modern life. Some people think that they should practice magic every day and if they do not then they have no right to perform a spell in a certain season. Yet this is a wrong way to think as just like the moon we wax and we wane. We may fell more connected to one particular season than to another and so our magic comes easy then. We have such busy lives that it is hard to embrace and acknowledge magic every week. Yet by just smelling a flower, looking at the clouds, watching the night sky, tending to the garden, clearing the autumn leaves, spring cleaning the house, planning a summer holiday or eating a particular dish that can only be made in that season you are acknowledging the turning of the year. You do embrace the magic that every season brings.

In this book we have delved into the magic of winter. However, even though each season is unique there is something inherently magical about winter whether you live in the Northern or Southern Hemispheres. Winter brings snows, frosts, fog, and rain and in return we develop new ways to enjoy it from skiing, skating, creating snowmen and catching snowflakes on our tongues. The subsequent books of Spring, summer, and autumn also bring with them the spells, and magic which is inherent within them.

The seasons of our lives are wrapped in nature. Just as spring is new and life is new the seasons flow through our lives from one stage passing into another. That is why it is important by no matter how small a gesture to acknowledge these moments. Every snowflake is unique; every seed holds new life and every raindrop brings potential. These are the seasons and they are a part of you. Sow the seeds of magic and embrace the splendour of each season.

Blessed be.

> The seasons come, the seasons go.
> The web of life grows and grows.
> With each silken thread, a golden opportunity.
> A journey through life's festivities.

Winter Calendar of Festivals

December

1 December - Advent meaning 'coming' or 'arrival' - within December the four weeks before Christmas are Advent beginning on the 1st December. In Advent we can find Christingle a delightful Christian service especially for children. In Christingle the orange represents the world. The central part is an orange with jellied sweets on. In the centre of the orange is a candle to mean the light of the world. Surrounding the candle are usually jellied sweets, fruits or nuts which symbolise the good things in life or the fruits of the earth.

8 December - Bodhi Day - Day of enlightenment for Buddha.
11 December - Sol Invictus or the Invincible Sun
17 - 23 December - Saturnalia
20 - 31 - Yule
21 - 25 - Panacha Granapti - 3 day festival of Lord Ganesha
24 December - Christmas Eve
25 December - Christmas Day

26 December - Boxing Day
26 December – 1 January - Kwanza
31 December - New Year's Eve

January

First full moon in January Thor's Feast

Blue Monday anywhere from the 17th to the 25th January - most depressing day of the year

17 January Wassailing the Apple Trees
31 January 2014 Chinese New Year - Year of the Horse
28 January 2017 Chinese New Year - Year of the Rooster
25 January 2020 Chinese New Year - Year of the Rat

February

2 February Imbolc/Candlemas/Groundhog Day
5 February 2019 Chinese New Year - Year of the Boar/Pig
8 February 2016 Chinese New Year - Year of the Monkey
9 February 2016 Shrove Tuesday/Pancake Day/Mardi Gras

13 February 2018 Shrove Tuesday/Pancake Day/Mardi Gras
13 - 15 February Lupercalia A festival of health and fertility
14 February St Valentine's Day
16 February 2018 Chinese New Year - Year of the Dog
17 February 2015 Shrove Tuesday/Pancake Day/Mardi Gras
19 February 2015 Chinese New Year - Year of the Sheep
25 February 2020 Shrove Tuesday/Pancake Day/Mardi Gras
28 February 2017 Shrove Tuesday/Pancake Day/Mardi Gras
29 February 2016 Leap Day
29 February 2020 Leap Day

Dictionary of terms and festivals throughout the year

The Wheel of the Year in Magic

Beltane	30th April/1st May - May Day
Imbolc	2nd February - First Festival of Spring
Lammas	1st August - First Festival of the Harvest
Litha	20-22 June - Summer Solstice
Mabon	22/23 September - Harvest Festival - Autumn Equinox
Ostara	21st March - Spring Equinox
Samhain	31st October - Celtic New Year
Yule	21/22 December - Winter Solstice

Online Course – Wicca 101

If this book has triggered something within and you wish to learn more about magic, spells and the earth then there is an online course for witchcraft which accompanies this series of books.

There are many different types of witchcraft but the branch of Wicca this course will teach is that of a hereditary tradition which is passed down within a family system. It is Celtic in origin stemming from various ancestors of Scottish, Irish and Welsh magical traditions. As such some words and phrases and names of herbs and plants will be in the old language but the English translation will also be given alongside.

Furthermore, there are degrees of witchcraft just as with any form of knowledge; there is a beginner, a graduate, and lastly, a teacher. There are therefore three levels within witchcraft and it is similar to university in that the second level is split into two, with lower second and upper second. In each of these levels there are symbols that witches use to describe the level they are.

This course is the first level of witchcraft. The first degree symbol is the inverted triangle; ▽ It shows that the novice or neophyte has been introduced to the most basic teachings and traditions. This shape is also drawn in the air as the threefold salute.

The lower second stage of witchcraft is a deeper level of knowledge. The symbol is an upright triangle △.

While the upper second level of witchcraft is the fivefold salute and it is the degree most witches stop at. The symbol is that sign which many acquaint with magic and witchcraft for it is the most magical symbol of all; the pentagram

In our tradition the pentagram is always upright. ☆ Think of the image of a human being with their arms and legs stretched outright. The Vitruvian man by Leonardo Da Vinci, who believed the workings of the human body to be an analogy of the workings of the universe; correspondences.

Incidentally, Da Vinci also wrote an accompanying text on the diagram in mirror writing. The text is in two parts, above and below the image - which is something we will delve deeper into; as above so below.

'Magic is all around us in every form.'
Tudorbeth

The third and final degree of witchcraft is that of the teacher or priest/priestess. It is the symbol of a pentagram which is surmounted by an upright triangle; see below.

This course is the first degree of witchcraft and by taking this course in Hereditary Wicca you are beginning a journey of knowledge that will be with you forever. As becoming a witch means you will always be a witch, chances are you have been one in previous life and now you have a longing to return home.

Witchcraft Course Outline

First Degree Level

△

The Beginning

Objective:

To learn what it means to be a witch.

To be able to cast your own spells.

To develop your knowledge of correspondences.

To realise your magical dreams and affirm them.

To gain techniques to help you with the development of potions and other magical resources.

To learn the fundamentals of witchcraft and our history.

Course Duration:

12 lessons which can be taught over 12 months depending on the needs and requirements of the student therefore the course can be longer but no shorter.

YOU CANNOT BECOME A WITCH IN A WEEK!

You must experience life as a witch for a year before you make that final decision. It is no easy choice. At the end of this course you can call yourself a witch but remember:

ONCE A WITCH ALWAYS A WITCH!

Course Teaching Methods:

Online course, online support, online coven. Series of 12 lessons with materials for each lesson supplied by Tutor. Interactive notice board for students to raise questions and theories.
Lessons will have tasks and activity for students to do in their own time and to email back to Tutor.

Course Equipment:

Book of Shadows/Grimoire

This can be anything from a simple exercise book to a highly decorative note book or a diary. It is for your personal use only; never let others see your Grimoire for it is sacred to the witch who owns it. The Book of Shadows or Grimoire is used to record your feelings, your dreams, spells, spells, potions, the festivals of the passing year, rituals and correspondences. It is essentially your personal own guidebook for witchcraft. You are beginning a journey and this book is a record of that journey.

NB: Though each lesson will come complete with its own course materials including the back ground reading required and the task.

Further, in addition to the course materials there are articles for each month of the year which contain the history, magical rites, and also spell for that month. The student can access these and learn alongside the course in relation to each corresponding month.

Outline of Course:

Initial Assessment

What does being a witch mean to you?

Write as much or as little as you want while answering the questions. It can be in any format from a list, to a poem, or a piece of prose. Think about everything you feel, heard, or remember when you hear or see the word witch.

Lesson 1
So you want to be a witch!
What does it mean to be a witch?
Are you sure this is the path you want to walk?
What is witchcraft?
What kind of witchcraft is this course?

Lesson 2
The History of Witchcraft

Who, where, when and why?
Destroying the stereotype.

Lesson 3
Magic, Magic Everywhere

How our societies are built upon magic in every form.

Lesson 4
Good v Bad

The debate on negative and positive witches. Protection spells. When to perform rituals.

Lesson 5
The Magical Year

The Wheel of The Year for witches. The correspondences for each festival and rituals to perform.

Lesson 6
Let's Go Shopping

What does a shopping list look like for a witch? What are the necessary things you need?

Lesson 7
Let's Begin!
Correspondences of nature, time and space.

Lesson 8
Gods, Goddesses - Yes or No

Do you feel the need to worship or work for a deity in your magical life or do you feel you can go it alone?
The pros and cons of deity worship.

Lesson 9
Spells

How to write a spell.
Cast a spell and watch what happens.

Lesson 10
Potions

What is a potion?
How to make a potion.
The Witches Flying Potion of history.

Lesson 11

Ritual

Writing and performing your own rituals.

Esbat and Sabbaths - what are they and the power they bring.

Lesson 12

Welcome to the Club!

Learning the initiation ceremony and performing it.

Why, how and when to perform the initiation ceremony.

Formative Assessment

Write how you feel now after completing the course.

Has your life changed any since beginning the course?

How to Find Out More

If you are interested in this course or you would like to find out more about the positive side to Witchcraft go to www.TudorPublishing.com and select Courses OR register for our updates at www.TudorPublishing.com/register.html

Bibliography

Binney, Ruth

    Wise Words & Country Ways: Weather Lore. David & Charles - 2010

    Wise Words & Country Ways: For Cooks. David & Charles - 2008

    Wise Words & Country Ways: For Gardners. David & Charles - 2007

    Wise Words & Country Ways: For House & Home. David & Charles 2000

Castleden, Rodney

    The Element Encyclopaedia of the Celts: The ultimate a-z of the symbols, history and spirituality of the legendary Celts. Harper Collins 2012

Conway, D.J.

    Norse Magic: Llewellyn Publications - 1990

    Celtic Magic: Llewellyn Publications - 1990

Day, Brian

    A Chronicle of Folk Customs: Octopus Publishing Group Ltd - 1998

Duggan, Ellen
>Autumn Equinox: The Enchantment of Mabon: Llewellyn Publications 2005

Eason, Cassandra
>The New Crystal Bible: Carlton Books Ltd - 2010

Forty, Jo
>Classic Mythology: Grange Books PLC - 1999

Harding, Mike
>A Little Book of The Green Man - Aurum Press Ltd 1998

Hedley, Christopher, and Shaw, Non
>Herbal Remedies: A practical beginner's guide to making effective remedies in the kitchen. Parragon Book Service Ltd - 1996

Houdret, Jessica
>A Visual Dictionary of Herbs: A Comprehensive Botanical A-Z Reference to Herbs. Anness Publishing Ltd - 2000

Kershaw, Stephen P.
> The Greek Myths: Gods, Monsters, Heroes and the Origins of Storytelling. Constable & Robinson Ltd - 2007

Leland, C.G.
> Aradia: Gospel of the Witches. David Butt - 1899

Macbain, A.
> Celtic Mythology and Religion. Sterling Enae Mackay - 1917

March, Jenny
> The Penguin Book of Classical Myths. Penguin Books - 2008

Mathews, John
> The Quest for the Green Man. Quest Books - 2001

Meadows, Kenneth
> The Little Library of Earth Medicine: Wolf. DK Publishing - 1998

Michael, Pamela
> Edible Wild Plants and Herbs. Ernest Benn - 1980

Moorey, Teresa

    The Fairy Bible. Octopus Publishing Group – 2008

Nozedar, Adele

    The Element Encyclopaedia of Secret Signs and Symbols: The ultimate a-z guide from alchemy to zodiac. Harper Element - 2008

O'Rush, Claire

    The Enchanted Garden. Random House - 2000

Palmer, Martin & Nigel

    Sacred Britain: A Guide to the Sacred Sites and Pilgrim Routes of England, Scotland and Wales. Piatkus - 1997

Purton, Rowland

    Festivals and Celebrations. Basil Blackwell Publisher - 1981

Tudorbeth

    The Craft in the City. Local Legend - 2012
    The Witch in the City. Local Legend - 2013
    Magic in the City. Local Legend. 2013
    Spirit in the City. Local Legend – 2013

Waterfield, Robin
> The Greek Myths: Stories of the Greek Gods
> and Heroes Vividly Retold. Quercus - 2013

Tudor Publishing

Tudor Publishing is an imprint of Aranon Publishing

www.aranonpublishing.com

Other titles published include:

ALTERNATIVE PRACTISES

The Dowsing Companion

Learn Chart Dowsing

Learn Map Dowsing

The Learn Dowsing Handbook

PERSONAL DEVELOPMENT

The Science of Being Great

The Science of Being Rich

The Science of Being Well

Introduction to NLP

Magical Relationships

Presenting for Profit

MAGIC & WITCHCRAFT

Seasons, Spells & Magic – SPRING

Seasons, Spells & Magic – SUMMER
Seasons, Spells & Magic – AUTUMN
Seasons, Spells & Magic - WINTER

OTHER

The Safety Handbook for Lone Women Travellers
The Little Book of Spiritual Quotes

AUDIOBOOKS

A Shot in The Arm (NLP)
An Introduction to NLP
Change Your Mood in an Instant
Create Empowering Beliefs (NLP)
Create Empowering Meanings (NLP)
Create Your Day (NLP)
Develop A Positive Attitude
Effective Goal Setting
Effective Time Management
Get The Edge in Selling (15 Minutes to Sell Series)
Magic Minutes
Magical Relationships

Mind Magic & Manifestation

Mind Switch

Overcome The Fear of Selling (15 Minutes to Sell Series)

Prioritising Tasks

Well-Formed Outcomes

Self-Hypnosis

Seven Keys to Asking The Right Questions (15 Minutes to Sell Series)

Slim Secrets

The Key Aspects of a Presentation

THINk by David Green

Turn Pain into Pleasure (NLP)

Understanding Karma

Ultimate Power Mind Tools

Waking The Gatekeeper

Your Personal Audit

Your Questions Define You (15 Minutes to Sell Series)

Don't forget to register your copy of this book online and gain access to Tudorbeth's Reader Resources at:

http://www.SeasonsSpellsandMagic.com

Printed in Great Britain
by Amazon